𝔄 𝔖𝔥𝔬𝔯𝔱 ℭ𝔞𝔱𝔢𝔠𝔥𝔦𝔰𝔪

ON CONFIRMATION

BY THE

REV. J. K. TUCKER, B. A.,

ST. PETER'S COLLEGE, CAMBRIDGE,

AND RECTOR OF PETTAUGH, SUFFOLK.

———

"The answer of a good conscience towards God."
1 *Peter* iii. 21.

———

Second Edition, Enlarged.

IPSWICH:

PRINTED AND SOLD BY HUNT AND SON, TAVERN STREET.
LONDON: SIMPKIN, MARSHALL, AND CO.,
AND SEELEY, BURNSIDE, AND SEELEY, FLEET STREET.

1847.

Price 2d. each, or 1s. 6d. per doz.

Prepared for the use of the young persons of his Parish, who are candidates for Confirmation ; with an earnest prayer that, by God's blessing, it may promote their spiritual and temporal happiness in this life, and their salvation in the next.

June 1st, 1847.

CONFIRMATION.

Question. Can you tell me what Confirmation is?

Answer. It is the ceremony of laying on of the Bishop's hands upon those who have been baptized, and come to years of discretion.

Q. Who is the *Bishop** ?

A. The chief minister of the Church, who ordains other ministers to their offices, and governs the whole Church as well clergy as people.

Q. Why do the *Bishops* only, and not other ministers, lay on hands?

A. Because we read in the Acts (viii. chap. 14 to 17 verse,) that Philip, who was only a *Deacon,* could not do so; but the apostles, Peter and John, were sent from Jerusalem for that purpose.†

Q. Who is a *Deacon ?*

A. The *lowest minister* of the Church, who generally had charge of the alms for the poor, and sometimes preached and baptized, (Acts vi. 3—6.)

---

* The word " Bishop " means *Overseer*.   † Hooker B. V. ch. 66.

Q. Were there any other ministers in the Church in the apostles' days?

A. Yes, the Elders, or Presbyters,—now called Priests,—as those ordained by Titus, in Crete. (Titus i. 5.)

Q. Why is the ceremony of laying on of hands called CONFIRMATION?

A. Because the persons receiving it are *confirmed* in all the privileges of their Baptism, by being admitted to the full communion of the Church; and they themselves also *confirm* and ratify the vows and promises made in their names by their sponsors.*

Q. Then it appears there are *two* parts in confirmation.

A. Yes, there is that which the Bishop does, and that which the person being confirmed does.

Q. What is the *Bishop's* part in this ordinance?

A. The Bishop's part is to lay his hands on the person confirmed with prayer for the increase of God's Holy Spirit.

Q. Why does he lay his hands on the person's head?

A. To shew that it is *that particular* person for whom he prays, and to signify that God's

---

*In Baptism you were *presented*,—in Confirmation you come to "*present*" to the Lord. You here "confirm, etc."—*Bridges' Address on Confirmation.* Thus the *infant* Jesus at eight days old was presented in the rite of circumcision, and the *youth* Jesus at twelve years of age presented himself at the feast of the Passover.—*Simeon's Serv. Psalm* lvi. 12, *Luke* ii. 22.

"fatherly hand" is ever over those who are his true children to defend them.*

Q. But does not the Bishop give his blessing and the Holy Spirit by laying on his hands?

A. The Bishop does not *properly* bless, or give the Holy Ghost, to any one, except by *praying* for him; but when God is pleased to answer his prayer, he may be said, in a sense, to bless the person for whom he prays.†

Q. Then what the Bishop principally does is to pray for the person, that he may receive the Holy Ghost?

A. Certainly, — though he also admits him to the full communion of the Church, and a right to take the sacrament of the Lord's Supper. This is a great privilege and blessing to those who receive it worthily.

Q. But does not the Bishop ask the persons confirmed a question?

A. Yes, he asks them whether, now they are come to years of understanding, they are willing to renew their baptismal vow, and give themselves up in a perpetual covenant to God.

Q. What is the part of the *person confirmed* in this ordinance?

A. The person confirmed declares his consent to the promises made in his name at his baptism, and

* Hooker, B. V. ch. 66, and Coll. in the Order for Confirmation.
†Deut. x. 8—Hooker B. V. ch. 66, "to pray for others is to bless them for whom we pray." See also, Gen. xxvii. 23, 27.

therefore to the Bishop's question he seriously and solemnly answers, " I DO."

Q. But do not the congregation take any part in this ordinance?

A. Yes, they join in the prayers offered up, that God would be mercifully pleased to give to those confirmed His grace and Holy Spirit.

Q. But is it not a very solemn thing to renew our baptismal covenant, and to be confirmed?

A. Yes, indeed it is—nothing can be more solemn; because by so doing we declare ourselves to be as new creatures in Christ Jesus—truly serious decided Christians: we declare that old things have passed away with us, and all things have become new—that we have put off the old man with his deeds, and have put on the new man, which is created after God in righteousness and true holiness*—we engage to give up the world, Satan, and sin—we avow ourselves the true disciples of the Lord Jesus Christ—and solemnly promise, with God's grace, to live the remainder of our days in the constant observance of all God's holy commands. Besides this, it is expected that we should forthwith take the Lord's supper. Truly this is a very serious matter!

Q. What is meant by our renouncing the world, the flesh, and the devil, which we engage to do in our baptism?

Ephes. iv. 22, 24.

A. We mean that we will have nothing more to do with worldly company and amusements, etc. in which God's name is not honoured, and which draw away our hearts from heavenly things ; absenting ourselves in particular from those *places* and scenes where gambling, drinking, dissipation,. profaneness, and other sins and immoralities are allowed. That we will strive to resist all those sinful desires and lusts of our nature which incline us to evil; as pride,* envy, impurity, drunkenness, immoderate anger, etc. and that we will watch against the temptations of Satan, and give up all those wicked deeds and habits which are practised and followed by his children—as blasphemy, lying, theft, and other sins.

Q. What do you mean by believing the articles of the Christian faith, which you also engage to do?

A. I mean that I firmly believe Jesus Christ to be the Son of God,—that he died for my sins,— and that he will bring all those who sincerely love Him to heaven.

Q. But do you not also profess to believe in God the Father and God the Holy Ghost?

A. Yes! I believe that God the Father made the world, and sent His Son to redeem mankind,†— and also I believe that God the Holy Ghost can alone sanctify and make me holy, and give me

*(See Gal. v. 19—21. 1 Tim. ii. 9, 10) Under *pride* may be comprehended the *love of dress* and shew, as the *exhibition of* this love is one of the pomps and vanities of the world which we promise to give up. †Acts xvii. 24—29. John iii. 16, 17.

strength to resist temptation,*—moreover, I believe that these Three Persons, the Father, the Son, and the Holy Ghost, are One God.†

Q. And what do you mean by "keeping God's holy will and commandments," as you also promise to do?

A. I mean that I make the ten commandments of God, called the "Moral Law," *my rule of life,* and that I will endeavour to obey them as far as I am able.‡

Q. Do you think that by keeping that law you will *deserve* salvation?

A. No, I know that I can be saved only by the merits and bloodshedding of my Lord and Saviour, Jesus Christ; and that with all my endeavours I cannot keep that law perfectly, and therefore cannot be saved by my obedience of it.§

Q. Do you not now think that it is a very sinful thing to go to confirmation in a thoughtless and trifling spirit, and to make the day a mere holiday, as so many do?

A. I do indeed! and I pray God I may go in a very different state of mind from that.

Q. Can you recollect any texts which describe the state of heart in which a person should go to be confirmed?

A. Yes, Isaiah xxvi. 13.; also Jer. l. 5.; and Deut. xxvi, 17.

*Rom. i. 4.   1 Cor. xii. 3.   Rom. viii. 13.   †Deut. vi. 4.   1 Cor. viii. 6.   2 Cor. 13, 14.   ‡Mark xii. 30.   Matt. v. 17, 19. §Rom. iii. 20—28.   Gal. ii. 16.

Q. What state of heart do these texts describe?

A. They describe a heart deliberately resolved to forsake the service of Satan, the world, and sin; sincerely disposed to love God above all things; and earnestly devoted to the constant service of its Saviour.

Q. Can you give any passages and examples from God's word which shew that the laying on of hands was a ceremony that followed baptism?

A. Yes, Acts viii. 14—17. Acts xix. 5, 6. Heb. vi. 2.

Q. Was not the Holy Spirit given in the use of the same form?

A. Yes, as appears by the texts above quoted.

Q. Was not the laying on of hands, with prayer, often used as a form of blessing?

A. Yes, Jacob used it, (Gen. xlviii. 14—16,) and Jesus used it to heal diseases, (Luke xiii. 13,) and in blessing little children (Mark x. 16).

Q. What do we learn from all this?

A. That the ceremony of confirmation is a scriptural form and ordinance, and that we may look for God's blessing upon it, if we use it aright.

Q. What do you think are the particular *uses* and *benefits* of this ordinance, which make it one that every Christian, who has been baptized in infancy, must feel it his duty and his privilege to observe it?

A. I look upon it as a most blessed *opportunity*

afforded me of confessing my Saviour publicly before the Church and the world, and declaring my faith as a Christian disciple, which, as I was too young to do it in my own name at my baptism, it is very fit I should do now, when I am come of age to do so.

Q. Is there no other use or benefit in this ordinance?

A. Yes, its most blessed use is, as it is a means for obtaining an increase of God's Holy Spirit, which I *daily* need. For not only must that Divine Spirit be given to us *once* that we may be *made* Christians, —as when at our Baptism, if received rightly,* we *commence* our Christian course,—but constant *renewals* of His grace in this† and other ordinances are needed, to strengthen and confirm us in that course, that so we may ever be *kept* and *continue* Christians.

Q. But does God give His Holy Spirit *only* at Baptism and the laying on of hands?

A. No, but also in answer to prayer, and in the use of all the means of grace—particularly the hearing and reading of His word.‡

Q. Can you think of no other use?

A. Yes, it affords an opportunity of my becoming known to my Bishop, and of my acknowledging his authority over me as my chief spiritual overseer.

Q. What do you mean by *overseer?*

A. A ruler, director, or manager. A *parish*

*Art. 27. †Confirmation Service, and Hooker B. V. ch. 66.
‡Prayer—Luke xi. 9—13. The Word of God—Ephes. vi. 17, v. 26.

overseer manages the affairs of the parish,—so does a Bishop the affairs of the Church, looking over the other ministers, depriving them of their offices if they do wrong, and punishing the lay members in like manner, by casting them out of the Church's communion for scandalous sins.

Q. You have not told me what are the *motives* which urge you take so solemn a step, as that of renewing your baptismal vow, renouncing the world, and dedicating yourself to the service of your Redeemer?

A. I do so because I feel it to be a Christian's "*reasonable service,*" * as a creature made and redeemed, preserved and sanctified for this very end and purpose—of glorifying his Creator; because also, I trust "the mercies of God," in creating, sustaining, and giving His Son to redeem me from His wrath,—"the love of Christ," in dying and being made a curse for me,†—and the grace and condescension of the Holy Spirit "in striving with" my evil heart,‡ notwithstanding my having so often grieved Him by my sins, "*constrain*" me to present my body as a living sacrifice, holy and acceptable unto so gracious a God,—"whose I am, and whom I ought to serve."§

Q. But are there not some other motives and reasons relating also to yourself, which move you

* Rom. xii. 1.

† 2 Cor. v. 14, 15.—Gal. iii. 13.   ‡ Gen. vi. 3.—evil heart, v. 5.

§ Acts xxvii. 23.

to this duty of presenting yourself to the Lord?

A. Yes, I know that to confess my Saviour before men,—to avow my trust in his precious blood-shedding and death as the only ground of my hope of pardon with God, and not to "be ashamed to confess the faith of Christ crucified," *is a duty requisite to my salvation*, as commanded by my Saviour,* and is moreover what was promised for me in my baptism. I know also, that unless I mortify my sinful lusts and tempers, and give up the world from my heart, I cannot be saved.†

Q. Then your motives are, a desire to glorify God, and to obey the command of Christ, in denying your evil nature for His sake, and confessing yourself His disciple, with a view to your salvation;—but may you not confess Christ in other ways beside being Confirmed?

A. Yes, I know I must do this *every day* of my life, by my holy walk and conversation as a Christian; but I know of no more fitting occasion—except that of taking the Lord's Supper—of doing so *publicly*, than the present, when invited by my Church to do so,—and I should feel that I had culpably slighted my Saviour, if I held back, through shame or a love of the world, and a desire to enjoy its guilty pleasures, when so many young persons in my neighbourhood were offering themselves to the Lord.‡

*Luke ix. 23, 26. †Rom. viii. 13. 1 John ii. 15—17. James iv. 4.
‡ Judges v. 23. See Wonston, Confirmation Tracts, No. iv.

Q. But I hope you do not undertake or expect to carry on this great work in reliance on your own strength; and that you have seriously counted the cost of serving the Lord fully? May I ask, do you think it an easy thing to be a Christian indeed; and by *what means* do you hope to "go forward"* in the difficult way you are now entering upon?

A. I trust I am fully conscious of my own utter weakness and insufficiency: that it is no easy matter to give up the world, subdue my fleshly nature, and follow Christ: and that it must be by earnest unceasing prayer to the Holy Spirit for His aid, and a diligent use of the means of grace, particularly the reading of the Scriptures, hearing the Gospel preached, and attending the Sacrament, that I can ever hope to prevail.

Q. What are those persons to expect who wilfully go back from their solemn engagements, and persist in a course of sin?

A. They can expect no less than *perdition,* as crucifying Christ afresh, and putting him to an open shame.†

Q. And what may they look for, who by God's grace "continue Christ's faithful soldiers and servants unto their life's end?"

A. It is their unspeakable happiness to look

* Ex. xiv. 15.   † Luke xvii. 32—Heb. vi. 4—8—and Heb. x. 26, 27, 39.

forward to a joyful and glorious eternity in God's presence.*

Well, I most earnestly pray that, as you are now about to be admitted to the privilege of full communion with God's people in His church, so you will ever hereafter, by God's grace, *continue* a faithful and devout member of it,—remembering the solemn caution of St. Paul to the Colossians, (i. chap. 23 v.) who intimates that such means and ordinances can only benefit you in the end: " If ye *continue* in the faith, grounded and settled, and be not moved away from the hope of the Gospel which ye have heard." You will find many things to move you away from that hope,—many temptations to unsettle you, and draw you aside from the narrow path on which you have now, I trust, begun to walk. But God will give you persevering grace, if you earnestly and diligently seek it of Him; I therefore subjoin a short prayer for your use.

* Heb. x. 35, 37. 1 Cor. ii. 9.

PRAYER.

———

"O Almighty God, who hast promised to give all grace to those who ask in thy Son's name, I beseech thee to hear the prayer of thy servant, who so much needs thy mercy and help : pardon all my past neglect and forgetfulness of the solemn promises, made at my baptism : assist me at this time to renew them with humility, seriousness, and devoutness : enlighten my understanding, that I may not through ignorance abuse this holy ordinance to my hurt : enable me, from this time, to give up the world, with its pomps and vanities : teach me my need of Christ, as my only and sufficient Saviour, and strengthen me by thy Holy Spirit to walk henceforth in all the commandments and ordinances of thy word blameless : I entreat these blessings at thy hand, O Lord, only for the merits of thy dear Son, Jesus Christ."

THE END.

HUNT AND SON, PRINTERS, IPSWICH.

CPSIA information can be obtained
at www.ICGtesting.com
Printed in the USA
LVRC021509291018
595206LV00016B/382

* 9 7 8 1 1 6 4 5 4 8 7 8 2 *